DOLPHINS!

STRANGE AND WONDERFUL

Laurence Pringle

Illustrated by
Meryl Henderson

BOYDS MILLS PRESS
AN IMPRINT OF HIGHLIGHTS
Honesdale, Pennsylvania

For Andrea and Greg Early, good friends and good people, who
for decades have worked on behalf of nature, especially ocean life
—LP

For my mother-in-law, Nellie Learnihan—a strong woman full of
faith, and generous with her healing prayers
—MH

The author and illustrator thank Dr. Randall Wells, Senior Conservation Scientist and Director
of Chicago Zoological Society's Sarasota Dolphin Research Program, based at Mote Marine
Laboratory, Sarasota, Florida, for his careful review of the text and illustrations.

Boyds Mills Press
An Imprint of Highlights
815 Church Street
Honesdale, Pennsylvania 18431
boydsmillspress.com
Printed in China

ISBN: 978-1-62979-680-2
Library of Congress Control Number: 2018937661

First edition
The text of this book is set in Goudy Oldstyle.
The illustrations are done in watercolor and pencil.

10 9 8 7 6 5 4 3 2 1

Dusky dolphin nursing her calf

If you were a young dolphin, your mother would keep you close, feed you milk, protect and teach you. Soon you would learn to swim fast and catch fish to eat. And sometimes you would leap from the water, high into the air!

If you were a dolphin, you would swim, hunt, and play with family members and with lifelong friends. You would be smart, and make an amazing variety of sounds—some to "talk" with other dolphins, some to help you catch food.

If you were a dolphin, you would be underwater nearly all of the time, hidden from human sight. People would be very curious about the secrets of your life beneath the surface.

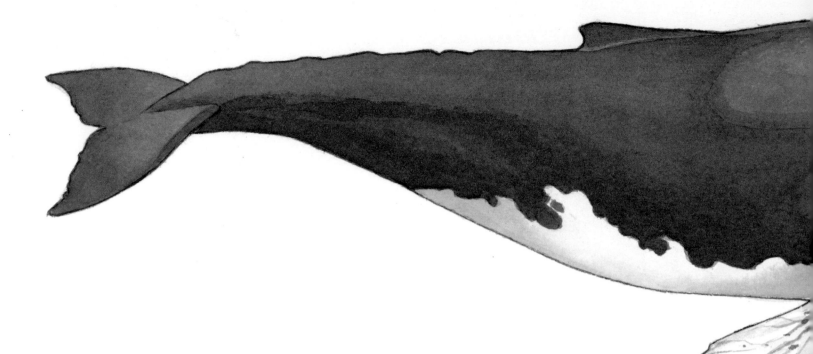

Dolphins live in all of Earth's oceans. They are **mammals**, which breathe air with lungs. They are also **cetaceans**, mammals that are adapted to live full time in water. (The word *cetacean* comes from Latin and means "large sea creature.") Whales and porpoises are also cetaceans.

Some kinds of whales are huge—bigger than any animals that live on land. All porpoises are small, measuring no more than eight feet long. And dolphins have quite a range of sizes, from four to thirty-two feet.

Oddly enough, six kinds of dolphins are called whales. Best known is the killer whale, also called *orca*, which is Earth's biggest dolphin. The other kinds of big dolphins with whale names are the pygmy killer whale, false killer whale, short-finned pilot whale, long-finned pilot whale, and melon-headed whale. These six species of dolphins are sometimes called **blackfish** because they have mostly black bodies.

Dolphins and porpoises look somewhat alike, but dolphins have longer, leaner bodies. Dolphins also have longer beaks and bigger mouths. The fin on the back of a porpoise, the **dorsal fin**, tends to be smaller and more triangular than that on dolphins. The teeth of porpoises and dolphins also differ. Dolphin teeth look like round pegs with sharp points. Porpoise teeth also have sharp points but are shaped like shovel blades.

Dolphin tooth

Porpoise tooth

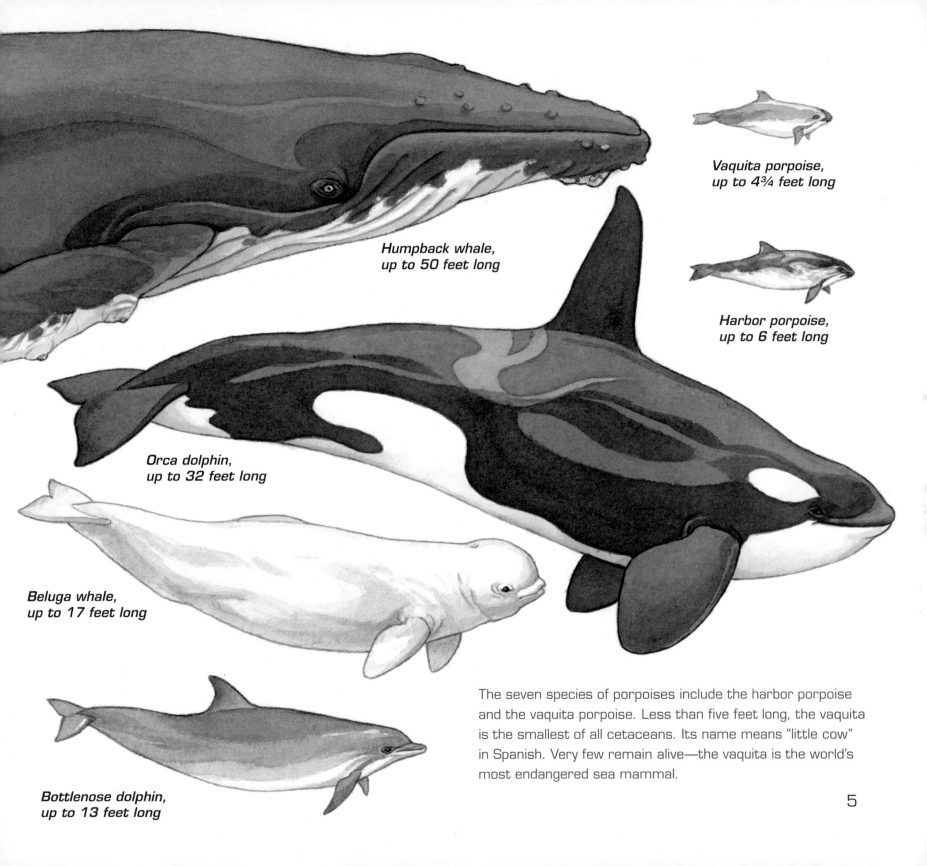

Vaquita porpoise,
up to 4¾ feet long

Humpback whale,
up to 50 feet long

Harbor porpoise,
up to 6 feet long

Orca dolphin,
up to 32 feet long

Beluga whale,
up to 17 feet long

The seven species of porpoises include the harbor porpoise
and the vaquita porpoise. Less than five feet long, the vaquita
is the smallest of all cetaceans. Its name means "little cow"
in Spanish. Very few remain alive—the vaquita is the world's
most endangered sea mammal.

Bottlenose dolphin,
up to 13 feet long

Dolphins vary a lot in their size, the color patterns on their bodies, and where they live. Some species are widespread, while others stay in a small area. For example, bottlenose dolphins swim in most oceans. By contrast, Hector's dolphin, the smallest species, lives only along some coasts of New Zealand.

Most dolphin species live in salty seawater, but a few have adapted to live in freshwater rivers.

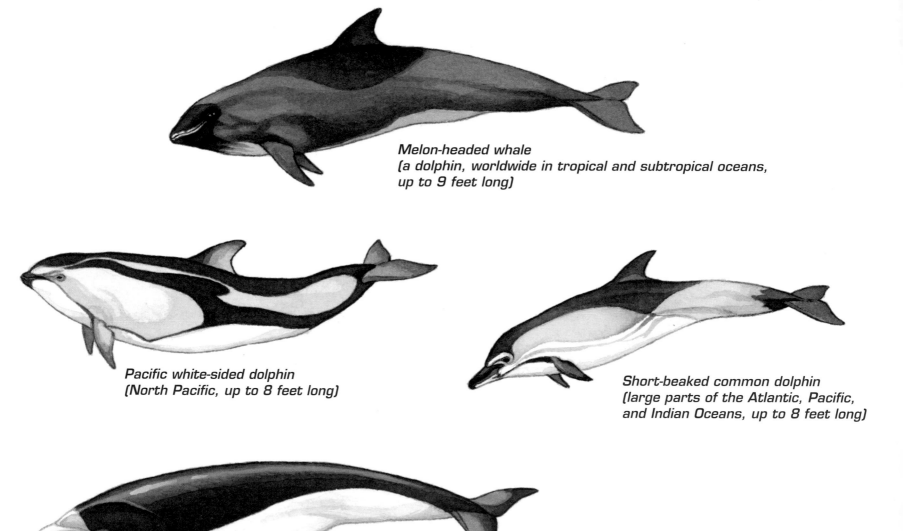

Melon-headed whale
(a dolphin, worldwide in tropical and subtropical oceans,
up to 9 feet long)

Pacific white-sided dolphin
(North Pacific, up to 8 feet long)

Short-beaked common dolphin
(large parts of the Atlantic, Pacific,
and Indian Oceans, up to 8 feet long)

Southern right whale dolphin
(lives in colder ocean waters of the Southern Hemisphere, up to 10 feet long)

Boto, or pink river dolphin
(Amazon and Orinoco Rivers of
South America, up to 9 feet long)

Rough-toothed dolphin
(worldwide in tropical and subtropical oceans,
up to 8½ feet long)

Eastern spinner dolphin
(tropical ocean waters, up to 8 feet long)

Atlantic white-sided dolphin
(North Atlantic, up to 9 feet long)

Risso's dolphin
(worldwide, up to 13 feet long)

7

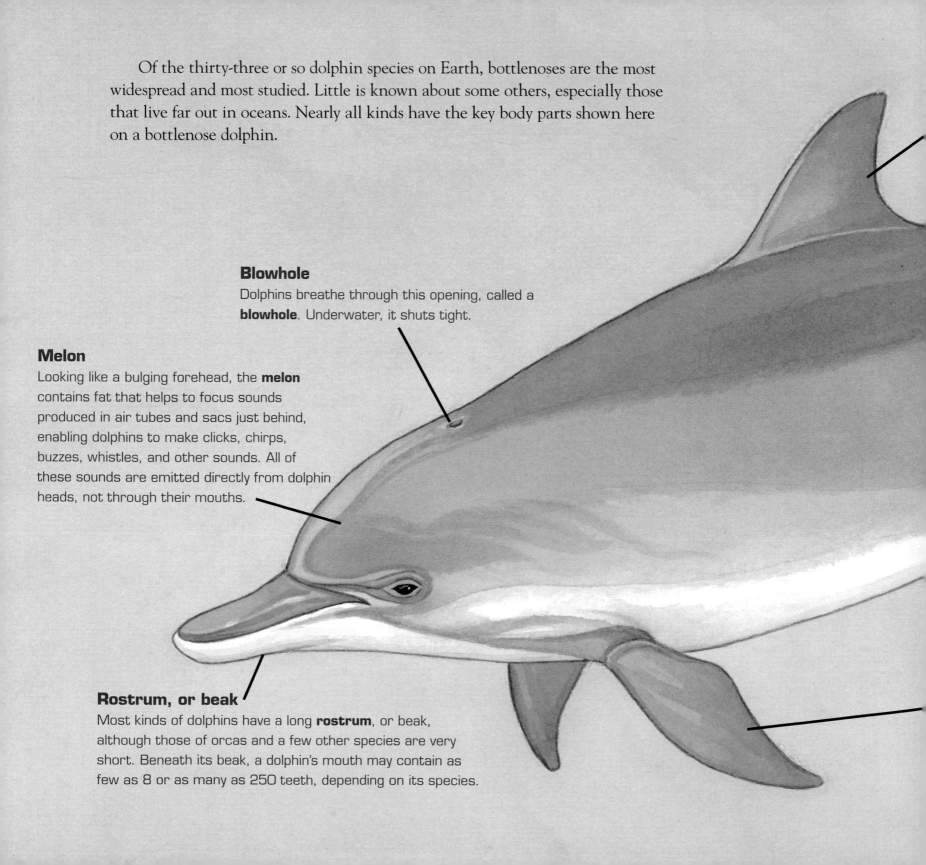

Of the thirty-three or so dolphin species on Earth, bottlenoses are the most widespread and most studied. Little is known about some others, especially those that live far out in oceans. Nearly all kinds have the key body parts shown here on a bottlenose dolphin.

Blowhole

Dolphins breathe through this opening, called a **blowhole**. Underwater, it shuts tight.

Melon

Looking like a bulging forehead, the **melon** contains fat that helps to focus sounds produced in air tubes and sacs just behind, enabling dolphins to make clicks, chirps, buzzes, whistles, and other sounds. All of these sounds are emitted directly from dolphin heads, not through their mouths.

Rostrum, or beak

Most kinds of dolphins have a long **rostrum**, or beak, although those of orcas and a few other species are very short. Beneath its beak, a dolphin's mouth may contain as few as 8 or as many as 250 teeth, depending on its species.

Dorsal fin

Most dolphin species have one large fin on top of their backs, though its shape varies by species. The dorsal fins of river dolphins are much smaller than those of other species. Southern and northern right whale dolphins have none.

Skin

Dolphin skin feels smooth and rubbery. Just under the skin is a layer of fat, called **blubber**, that helps keep a dolphin warm in cold water. The blubber may also protect the dolphin by keeping a shark's teeth from cutting deep into its body.

Flukes

Powerful muscles move a dolphin's tail fins, called **flukes**, to push its body through water. Flukes move up and down, unlike a fish's tail, which swings from side to side.

Flippers

A dolphin's two front **flippers** (pectoral fins) are vital for steering and turning in the water.

Striped dolphins porpoising

Dolphins can swim fast and some can dive deep. Their streamlined bodies quickly slice through the water. Zooming along, they take long, low leaps out of the water. Swimming fast this way is called **porpoising**. Most kinds of dolphins usually travel at about two to four miles an hour. However, if they need a quick burst of speed, such as while chasing prey, they can go more than twenty miles an hour. (The fastest speed at which humans can run is about twenty-eight miles an hour for short distances.)

Dolphins sometimes leap completely out of the water. This is called **breaching**. Dusky dolphins breach much more often than other species. Long-snouted spinner dolphins are called spinners because they twirl around in the air—up to seven spins in one leap.

Dolphins spend most of their lives underwater, and can go for many minutes without needing to breathe. Their lungs are rather small for the size of their body, but they can store vital oxygen in their blood and muscles. Diving deep to hunt for food, some dolphins hold their breath for seven or eight minutes, and sometimes longer. In that time, it might dive 200 or more feet beneath the surface. Judging from the deep-water fish found in their stomachs and from tracking devices attached to their fins, some dolphins catch food more than 1,700 feet below the surface.

Dusky dolphin breaching

Dolphin Breathing and Sleeping

As you read these words, you don't need to think about breathing. It happens automatically. A dolphin, on the other hand, decides when to breathe. But how can it sleep and still keep breathing? The answer: One side of its brain rests while the other stays awake. Half-asleep, the dolphin rises to the surface to breathe.

Underwater at many places around the world, it is often hard to see clearly, so dolphins use sounds and a keen sense of hearing to find food and to find their way. They rely on a system called **echolocation**. Here is how it works:

From its head, a dolphin sends out beams of clicking sounds—as many as seven hundred clicks per second. The clicks include sounds that are too high-pitched for humans to hear. In water or air, sound travels as invisible waves. The sound waves from a dolphin might bounce off the seabed, an underwater object, or a school of fish. Echoes of the clicks return to the dolphin.

The dolphin does not detect sounds with its ears. Dolphins listen with their chins! Echoes are received by thin bones in their lower jaws and sent through channels of fat to their inner ear bones. Then information from the echoes is sent to their brains. This gives them a picture of what lies ahead.

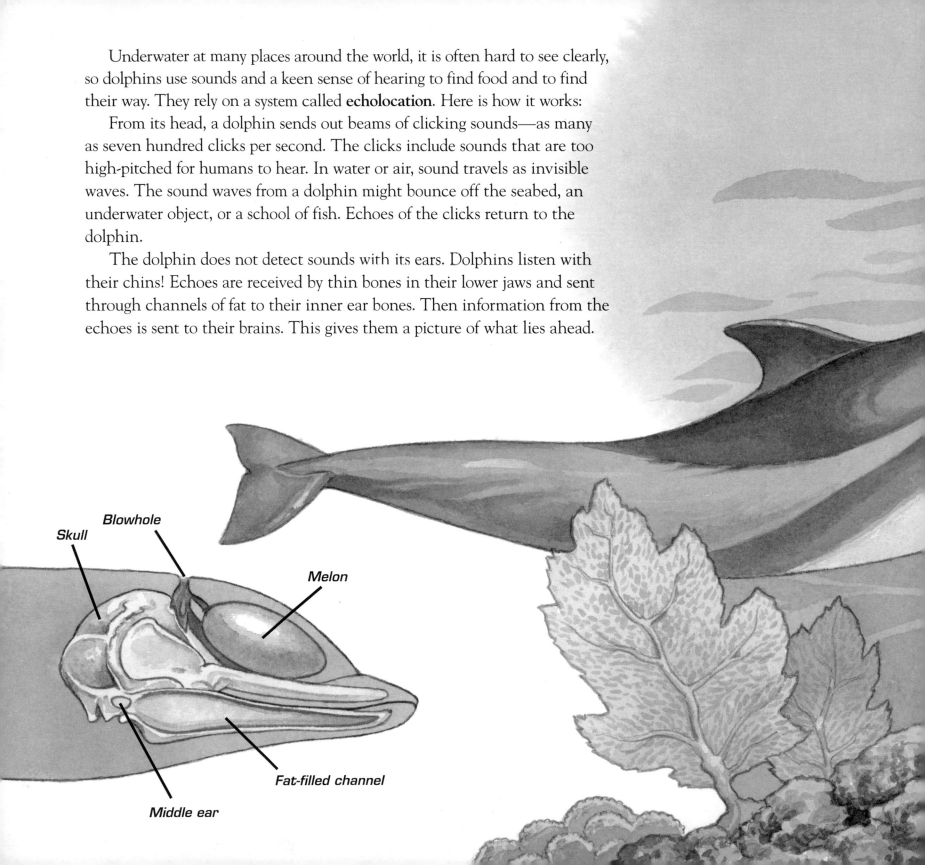

Skull

Blowhole

Melon

Fat-filled channel

Middle ear

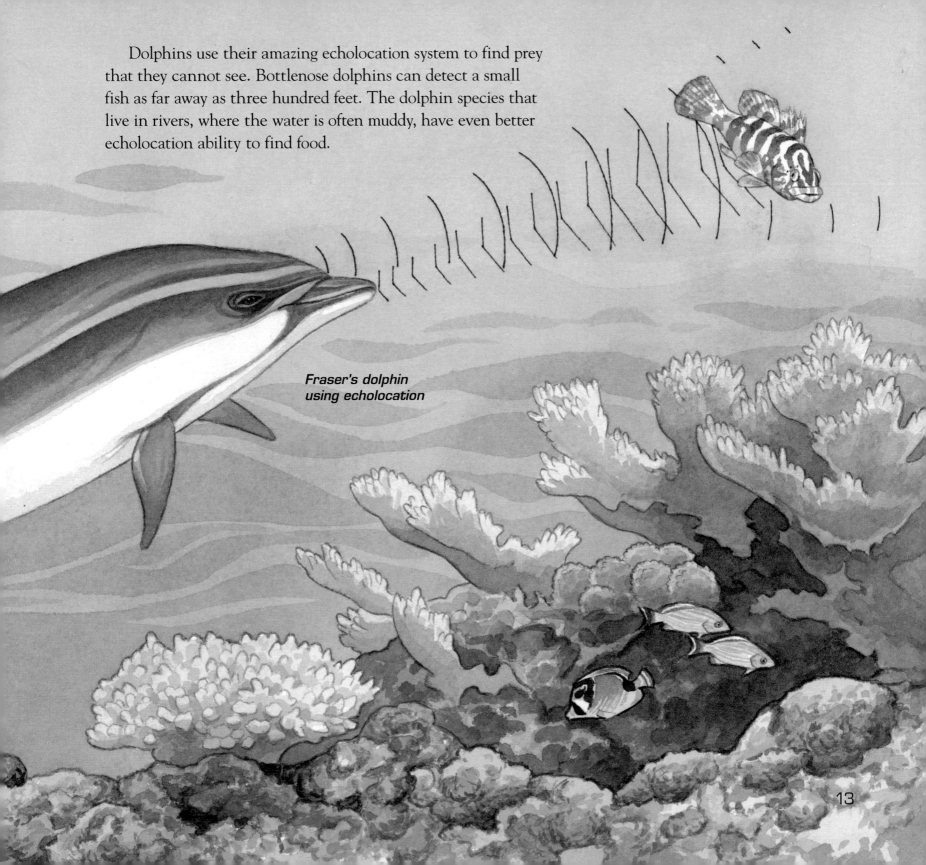

Dolphins use their amazing echolocation system to find prey that they cannot see. Bottlenose dolphins can detect a small fish as far away as three hundred feet. The dolphin species that live in rivers, where the water is often muddy, have even better echolocation ability to find food.

Fraser's dolphin using echolocation

13

Dolphins are **predators**. They eat other animals. Swimming in water requires more energy than moving on land, so dolphins must eat a lot, every day. Some species always hunt far out in oceans; others stay close to coasts. And dolphins that live in sheltered bays must at times venture into deeper ocean water to find their prey.

Dolphin teeth grab and hold onto fish and other slippery prey. They don't chew their food. They gulp it down whole, or tear it into pieces and then swallow. Most dolphins eat fish, but different species hunt a variety of prey. Spinner dolphins hunt mainly at night, and catch small fish, squid, and shrimp. White-beaked dolphins hunt mainly in the day, and eat fish, octopuses, and crustaceans. A few dolphins kill and eat porpoises, and even other kinds of dolphins. And orcas, the biggest of all dolphins, may attack such large prey as sea lions, sharks, sea turtles, and whales.

Some of the different ways dolphins catch food are shown on this and the next three pages.

Pacific white-sided dolphins

A **school** of hunting dolphins acts like a team. When one dolphin detects a school of fish or squid, the whole group encircles it. They swim closer and closer until the prey forms a tight bunch. Then the dolphins take turns, darting in to feed.

15

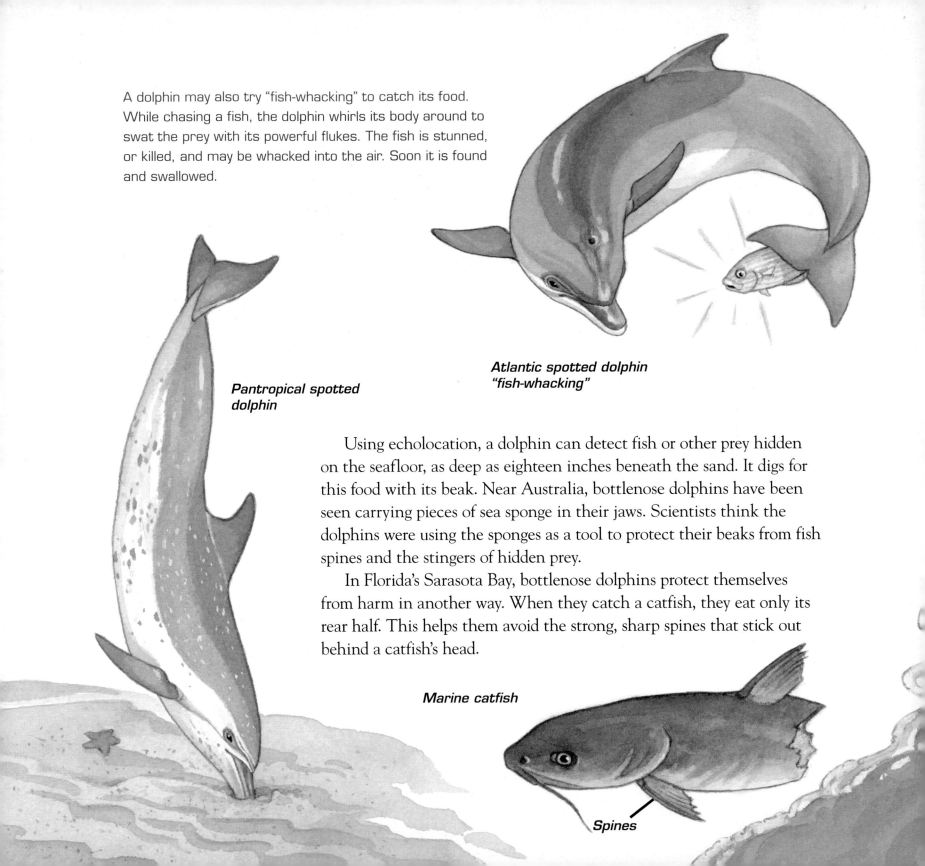

A dolphin may also try "fish-whacking" to catch its food. While chasing a fish, the dolphin whirls its body around to swat the prey with its powerful flukes. The fish is stunned, or killed, and may be whacked into the air. Soon it is found and swallowed.

Atlantic spotted dolphin "fish-whacking"

Pantropical spotted dolphin

Using echolocation, a dolphin can detect fish or other prey hidden on the seafloor, as deep as eighteen inches beneath the sand. It digs for this food with its beak. Near Australia, bottlenose dolphins have been seen carrying pieces of sea sponge in their jaws. Scientists think the dolphins were using the sponges as a tool to protect their beaks from fish spines and the stingers of hidden prey.

In Florida's Sarasota Bay, bottlenose dolphins protect themselves from harm in another way. When they catch a catfish, they eat only its rear half. This helps them avoid the strong, sharp spines that stick out behind a catfish's head.

Marine catfish

Spines

Orcas and bottlenose dolphins sometimes herd prey into shallow water, or even onto a sloping beach. The dolphins may even slide onto muddy shorelines to grab prey, then wriggle back into the water.

Bottlenose dolphins

17

Dolphins are great communicators. They use touch, body movements, and a great variety of sounds to relate to one another—and to other creatures. A mother dolphin, for example, may protect her young by sending bursts of sound to scare away a shark. Dolphins can also make two different sounds at the same time. While sending out chirps and whistles in dolphin "talk," they continue sending streams of clicks for echolocation.

Some dolphin species don't make whistling sounds. In most kinds, however, a young dolphin creates its own **signature whistle**. It is like a name. Other dolphins learn and remember the sound. Even when two dolphins have been apart for years, they recognize one another by their special whistles.

According to a Canadian scientist, orca dolphins at play emit "burbles, squeals, whistles, raspberries, and snorks."

Orca

Commerson's dolphins

Dolphins also send messages with their bodies. They rub against the skin of other dolphins, and touch flippers with them. Sometimes dolphins hit, ram, and bite each other. This can be playful behavior, but it can also be a sign of aggression.

When a dolphin is well fed, or feels safe or playful, it often leaps out of the water. A dolphin searching for prey may give a special leap that says, "I found food here." A tail slap on the surface can also send a message. For example, a mother dolphin's tail slap can tell her young, "Pay attention! Come here!"

Dolphins are very social animals. They live in groups called schools, usually made of twenty or fewer individuals. However, when a great supply of food is found far out at sea, several thousand spinner dolphins may gather together in one huge group. Sometimes a big mixed group of several dolphin species hunt together.

Whether in a large or a small group, dolphins usually watch out for one another. While some rest, others stay alert for danger. If one dolphin is sick or wounded, it gives a special whistle, a call for help. Other dolphins may use their bodies and flippers to lift that dolphin to the surface so it can breathe.

Bottlenose dolphins are known to make lifelong friendships, although they often live in different schools at different stages of their lives. For example, females with young of the same age keep together or repeatedly spend time together. Adult males form a strong pair-bond and travel and hunt together. Another kind of dolphin school is made up of **sub-adults**. They are several years old, and interact with each other in changeable, fluid groups until they are fully grown. Dolphins need ten years, and sometimes longer, to be fully grown. During this time, males may form strong bonds. Two sub-adult males may become buddies for their whole lives.

Short-beaked
common dolphins

A Dolphin Pod Is Not a Dolphin School

Unlike other kinds of dolphins, which live in schools, orcas
live in close-knit family groups called **pods**. A pod contains
one or two adult females and all of their young, both males
and females. Even when young orcas become adults, they
stay with their mothers for life.

Dolphins—young and old—are famous for their playfulness. They leap, chase, splash, and frolic together. Some play with their food, pieces of seaweed, or other objects. Dolphins seem to enjoy sneaking up on gulls, pelicans, and other creatures just to surprise them. Dolphins under human care create and play with rings, spirals, or curtains of bubbles. Many wild dolphins seem to love **bow-riding** or **wake-riding**—surfing on waves created by a boat or ship in motion. This makes travel easier, but they also seem to do it just for fun.

Short-snouted spinner dolphins

22

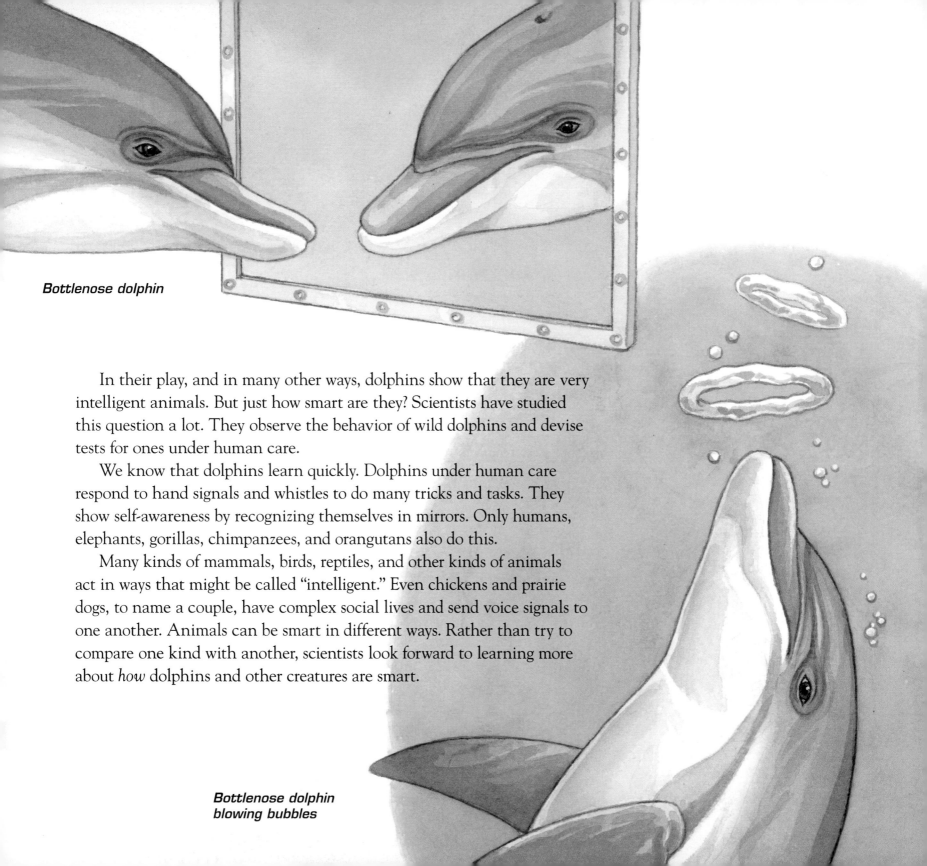

Bottlenose dolphin

In their play, and in many other ways, dolphins show that they are very intelligent animals. But just how smart are they? Scientists have studied this question a lot. They observe the behavior of wild dolphins and devise tests for ones under human care.

We know that dolphins learn quickly. Dolphins under human care respond to hand signals and whistles to do many tricks and tasks. They show self-awareness by recognizing themselves in mirrors. Only humans, elephants, gorillas, chimpanzees, and orangutans also do this.

Many kinds of mammals, birds, reptiles, and other kinds of animals act in ways that might be called "intelligent." Even chickens and prairie dogs, to name a couple, have complex social lives and send voice signals to one another. Animals can be smart in different ways. Rather than try to compare one kind with another, scientists look forward to learning more about *how* dolphins and other creatures are smart.

Bottlenose dolphin blowing bubbles

Peale's dolphins

As the first sentence of this book says, mother dolphins do it all: feeding, protecting, and teaching their young. Father dolphins are no help. After mating, they leave.

Female dolphins are often about ten years old before they are fully grown and able to breed. For most species, a full year after mating is needed for a baby (**calf**) to develop within its mother. Orcas need sixteen months. (For a human baby, this **gestation period** is about nine months.) A newborn calf needs to start breathing right away. It usually rises to the surface by itself to take its first breath or may be lifted there by its mother.

A young calf stays very close to its mother, often right by her dorsal fin. The mother's strong swimming makes it easier for the calf to go through the water, which saves the calf's energy.

To nurse, the calf holds its breath and goes underwater. It sticks its beak into one of two slits in its mother's belly for quick bursts of rich milk. A calf grows fast. It nurses milk for at least a year and often longer, but in a few months also starts to catch and eat fish. It usually stays near its mother for several years.

Calves watch, listen, and learn. They are "homeschooled" by their mothers. Schools of mothers and their calves often stay in areas of shallow water, which are safer for them than deep waters. In Florida's Sarasota Bay, groups of bottlenose dolphin mothers sometimes circle around, patrolling the edges of a "playpen" for their young. Play helps the calves become better swimmers, leapers, and hunters.

In a few years, calves leave their mothers and join a sub-adult group. With luck, bottlenose dolphins can live to fifty or sixty years or more. Females live longer than males. Some females in their late forties still give birth and raise calves. With wisdom from long experience, they often make the best mothers.

White-beaked dolphins and great white sharks

Some land animals can escape from predators by climbing a tree, or hiding in a burrow. Dolphins have no place to hide. They're always out in the open. Their main natural enemies are big sharks, especially tiger, bull, and great white sharks. These sharks tend to go after easier prey: lone or injured dolphins, or calves that stray too far from their mothers. Nevertheless, many adult dolphins have scars from shark bites on their bodies or fins.

Other dangerous predators of dolphins are other dolphins. Most deadly are a type of roaming orcas, called **transients**, that prey on dolphins and whales. However, they aren't the only deadly dolphins. Although people think of dolphins as always peaceful, cooperative creatures, they are also killers—and not just for food. Sometimes male dolphins kill calves of their own species. And some male bottlenose dolphins kill smaller harbor porpoises.

Counter-shading helps dolphins hide from both predators and prey. Most species have dark backs and light-colored bellies. (So do many kinds of fish.) From above, a dolphin may be hard to see because its dark back blends in with deep, dark waters. From below, it may be hard to see because its light belly blends in with sky-lit water above.

Worldwide every year, about two thousand dolphins and other cetaceans die in **mass strandings**. Sometimes a few and sometimes many dolphins are stranded on a beach and can't get back to water. There is usually no clear evidence of what causes dolphins to swim up onto a beach, and there are many possible reasons. One possibility in some cases is that they are chased by orcas. Another is that one dolphin gets stranded, sends distress signals, and the rest of its group comes to help. Also, in some places dolphin echolocation may fail to work. Dolphins may mistake a gently sloping beach for deeper water.

27

The worst enemies of dolphins, by far, are humans. In several places, including Japan, people hunt dolphins for food. In Peru, fishermen kill thousands of dolphins each year to use as bait for sharks. Many dolphins also drown when they accidentally get tangled in nets set for fish and can't reach the surface to breathe. Changes in net design and ways of fishing have helped reduce these losses.

Long-snouted spinner dolphin

28

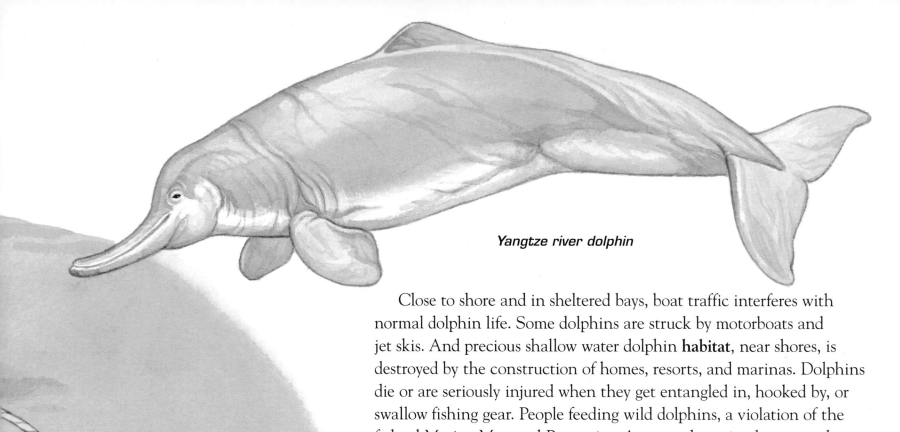

Yangtze river dolphin

Close to shore and in sheltered bays, boat traffic interferes with normal dolphin life. Some dolphins are struck by motorboats and jet skis. And precious shallow water dolphin **habitat**, near shores, is destroyed by the construction of homes, resorts, and marinas. Dolphins die or are seriously injured when they get entangled in, hooked by, or swallow fishing gear. People feeding wild dolphins, a violation of the federal Marine Mammal Protection Act, put the animals at great harm from being attracted to human activities.

Dolphins are also harmed by pollution from industries, agriculture, and human wastes. Harmful chemicals become stored in blubber and can be passed on to nursing calves. In the world of dolphins, even loud sounds can be a kind of pollution. Underwater noise from ships can temporarily keep dolphins from hearing the sounds they need to hear in everyday life.

Water pollution and heavy boat traffic is often at its worst in rivers. These factors, plus illegal fishing, caused the **extinction** of China's Yangtze river dolphin. None have been seen since 2002. In India and Pakistan, the Indus and Ganges river dolphins are also in danger of extinction. Boto dolphins of South American rivers are still fairly plentiful, but are killed illegally by fishermen to be sold as fish bait. Worldwide, several kinds of dolphins and porpoises are threatened by extinction.

Many nations, including the United States, have passed laws to protect dolphins and other cetaceans, though enforcing the laws can be a challenge.

Dolphins have fascinated people for thousands of years. They are pictured on coins and in the art of ancient Greece and Rome. In legends, dolphins are often powerful allies and helpers of humans. And today, people continue to find dolphins appealing. Many imagine them as always playful and friendly. Dolphins even seem to smile at us!

In fact, scientists say, dolphins do not smile. The bones and muscles of dolphin faces give them a look that resembles a human smile. Dolphins always have that look. A dolphin has it when it plays, and also when it tries to escape from a shark. A dolphin has it when it shows friendly behavior to a person, and also when it bites and rams a person.

People may learn the truth about dolphin smiles when they see dolphins under human care in aquariums. They may also learn safety rules during popular "swim with a dolphin" programs. For example, swimming directly at a dolphin can be dangerous. To a dolphin, that is like an attack. Swimming side by side is safer.

Research on dolphins under human care has helped scientists learn a lot that they could not have discovered in the wild. Some people, however, feel that dolphins should not be confined, especially to perform in aquatic shows. They campaign to end such shows. However, people who are entertained by watching live dolphins in action learn to appreciate them. They may develop a life-long commitment to protecting dolphins in the wild. Boat trips to watch dolphins are popular, but can sometimes disrupt normal lives of wild dolphins, and even injure some.

For thousands of years, humans have been curious about dolphins. We've learned a lot, but their lives still hold many mysteries. One thing we know for certain: if we want to have wild dolphins to appreciate and study, far into the future, people must do more to protect them and their habitats all over the world.

Ancient Syracuse coin

Glossary

blackfish—A name sometimes given to six species of dolphins—mostly black in color—including the largest dolphin of all, the orca, or killer whale.

blowhole—The nostril at the top of a dolphin's head, through which it breathes.

blubber—A layer of fat beneath the skin of dolphins (and other cetaceans). Blubber helps keep cetaceans warm in cold water, stores energy, and helps as armor against bites from sharks and cuts from boat propellers.

bow-riding—Surfing on the waves created at the bow (front) of a vessel moving through water. Sometimes dolphins also ride bow waves created by large whales.

breaching—Leaping partway or completely out of the water, then landing with a splash.

calf—A young dolphin. Female adult dolphins are sometimes called cows, and males are bulls.

cetaceans—Aquatic mammals in the scientific order Cetacea, including all dolphins, porpoises, and whales.

counter-shading—A color pattern of most dolphins and many fishes, with a dark back and a light underside. This pattern can help hide a dolphin from being seen from above or below.

dorsal fin—The fin on a dolphin's back that helps keep its body upright in the water.

echolocation—An ability of dolphins and of bats to send out sounds, then receive and learn from the returning echoes. This system of "seeing" with sounds enables dolphins to navigate, locate and catch food, and avoid enemies.

extinction—The end of a process in which every individual of a whole species dies and the species no longer exists.

flippers—A dolphin's front or pectoral fins, one on each side, which are vital for steering and turning. Flippers are also important in dolphin social life, as they often touch one another with their flippers.

flukes—The two fins at the end of the tail of a dolphin, porpoise, or whale.

gestation period—The length of time needed for a baby mammal to develop within its mother's body before birth.

habitat—The living place or environment where an organism normally exists.

mammals—Warm-blooded animals that give birth to live young whose mothers produce milk for their first food. Mammals also have hair, but in dolphins only newborn calves briefly have some whiskers on their upper jaws.

mass stranding—An often fatal event when a group of dolphins or other cetaceans swim onto a beach and are unable to get back to water.

melon—The bulging forehead of a dolphin, which contains fat-filled spaces that focus sound.

pods—Groups of orca dolphins, usually led by the oldest female, that are made up of several generations of orcas, all related to one another. In a pod, both male and female calves stay with their mothers for life.

porpoising—Fast travel by dolphins and porpoises that includes low leaps out of the water.

predators—Animals that kill and eat other animals for food.

rostrum—The front of a dolphin's head, including its jaws and teeth. Also called a beak.

school—A group of dolphins, usually fewer than twenty in number. At times many schools join to become a much larger group.

signature whistle—A specific sound that a young dolphin creates that is its alone.

sub-adults—Young dolphins, usually between seven and ten years of age (depending on the species), that are no longer with their mothers but not yet adults.

transient orcas—Populations of orcas that prey on seals, dolphins, whales, and other marine mammals as they roam the west coast of southern Alaska and southern Canada.

wake-riding—Surfing by dolphins in a boat's wake (waves created behind a moving vessel).

To Learn More

Books and periodicals

Barnes, Julia. *The Secret Lives of Dolphins*. Milwaukee, WI: Gareth Stevens, 2007.

Chadwick, Douglas H. "Investigating a Killer." *National Geographic*, April 2005, pp. 85–105.

Miller-Schroeder, Patricia. *Bottlenose Dolphins*. NY: Raintree Steck-Vaughn, 2002.

Montgomery, Sy. *Encantado: Pink Dolphin of the Amazon*. Boston: Houghton-Mifflin, 2002.

Morell, Virginia. "Feeding Frenzy." *National Geographic*, July 2015, pp. 77–89.

Pringle, Laurence. *Dolphin Man: Exploring the World of Dolphins*. Honesdale, PA: Boyds Mills Press, 1995.

Walker, Sally. *Dolphins*. Minneapolis, MN: Carolrhoda, 1999.

Websites* (for information about dolphins and their conservation)

acsonline.org (American Cetacean Society)
https://www.youtube.com/user/NationalGeographic/search?query=dolphin
https://www.youtube.com/user/BBCEarth/search?query=dolphin
dolphins.org (Dolphin Research Center)
dolphins-world.com
oceana.org
understanddolphins.com
sarasotadolphin.org
*Active at time of publication

Sources

The main sources of information for this book include the following books and articles, most written by dolphin researchers:

Cahill, Tim. *Dolphins*. Washington, DC: National Geographic, 2000.

Carwardine, Mark. *Whales, Dolphins, and Porpoises*. New York: Dorling Kindersley, 2002.

Dudzinski, Kathleen, and Toni Frohoff. *Dolphin Mysteries: Unlocking the Secrets of Communication*. New Haven, CT: Yale University Press, 2013.

Gregg, Justin. *Are Dolphins Really Smart? The Mammal behind the Myth*. London: Oxford University Press, 2013.

Morell, Virginia. "Can the Vaquita Be Saved?" *Science*, August 8, 2008, p. 767.

———. "Killer Whales Earn Their Name." *Science*, January 21, 2011, pp. 274–76.

Reeves, Randall R., Brent S. Stewart, Phillip J. Chapman, and James A. Powell. *Guide to Marine Mammals of the World*. New York: Knopf, 2002.

Simmonds, Mark. *Whales and Dolphins of the World*. Cambridge, MA: MIT Press, 2004.

Index